Princess from the Moon

Poetry

William Khalipwina Mpina

Publisher:
Footprints Publishing House
P.O. Box 30162
Chichiri
Blantyre 3
Malawi

Email: fpublishinghouse@gmail.com

Cell: +265884137788

ISBN: 9798652027612

TABLE OF CONTENTS

ACKNOWLEDGEMENTS

I wish to extend my gratitude to the editors of the following online literature magazines where some of the poems were published for the first time: Kalahari Review for *'The Evening'* and *'Wild Waves'* Nthanda Review for *'Rains'* and *'Postcard for Gumbi town'* Atunis Galaxy Poetry for *'The Graveyard blinks in season'* and *'Sleep Child'* Poetica Magazine for *'Python'* African Writer for *'Tantrums for a fallen hero'* and *'In pursuit of Identity, Integrity* and *Patriotism'*. And individuals such as Alfred Msadala, Egidio Mpanga, Temwani Mgunda, Benedicto Wokomaatani Malunga, Dr Nick Tembo for their positive feedback towards my attempt in writing.

The Evening

The evening comes when sleep is nullified
With blinking of cars dancing to a smiling dark cloud
Gaping and grudging of the furniture grieving outside.
The evening comes, upset
Tightly squeezed, skeptical about the beauty of life
Marred with winds of uncertainty
Songs bereft of the muse
Busy shining and painting white
Their necropolis masks
The evening comes tearing apart
The sinews of my heart

Wild waves

The floodgates of pleasure are shut
As waves rise against paradise tides
Wander through a forest of peace
Flood beauty with specks of wood
And wallow in freedom of blindness
No troubled mind beckon love
Only dry leaves whisper to each other
New songs of amorous tears
No face scowls at the stars
Only drum beats and flashes of light
Shoot the ugliness of the night
Truth dives deep into the cave of the heart
Submerges under the whimpering and whining
Of wild waves year in year out

Rains

Rains came boisterously.
Red water
Swept the road;
Rubbed off the ridges.
All the pools flooded;
Amid
Twinkling of lightning
And claps of thunder.
When all the water had gone
And the place was quiet
We danced in the mud.
...and when we danced
The minnows slipped;
Some into oblivion
While others like some stars
Did not depend on darkness to shine.

Python

Darkness upturned on the face
Of the midday light
Overwhelmed by breathtaking beauty
Of peace singing on its shores,
Sneaked into the womb of a long-term bond
And sat where the mouth of love dipped honey
Sagacity stumbling upon a basket
In casket of sanctity
Thought I saw an elephant's tusk
Swallowing sweet aroma of symphonic songs
Thought it was an insect's mouth kissing
The wet red mound of earth
No, it was a python begging me
To offer her a place next to the choir
I knew not it was a python
Because in the forest of her grandeur
Her footsteps hissed across the floor
Ushering everybody into an air of holiness
Coiled, brightened, elongated and clambered
Like feelers in my heart--
Embraced shadows of doubt
And sang her lungs out
In the evening, strong winds feasted

On her make-up, pulled out her long tail
From her miniskirt
She, laughing and smearing sores
Of my loneliness, slithered
Into my house spinning in circles
Kissing the ugliness of my past
Crestfallen, subjugated by wills and promises
Swim in fried pieces of advice
Stolen from the fridge of memory
While wind and dust buffeting my eyes

Tantrums for a Fallen Hero

Specks of dust danced in the twilight
In silence like hoofs of cattle
Men's feet forked out sand.
Behind them, women in black.
Their arms lazily dancing to
Tom-toms of their bottoms;
Two massive hills singing to the tune
Of their silent parade.
Squat, they did.
Meters away from the secluded house
Where hoes, a shovel, a pick and a Panga knife
Lined up to report that he indeed is gone
Gone to meet his ancestors
Slowly, a chief's aide walked towards
Them, and whispered a question to
The elderly man at the front who
Hissed a long rehearsed winding statement
About their walk

To and from the graveyard, about
Their feet stepping on ghosts-made ground
About black ghosts caressing their bald-heads
Invisible frogs spitting water to clean their feet
Crows like black angels flying above
The grave and about harmless bees
Buzzing friendlier than the chorister's voice.
Still squatting in a column, wait they had to
Till they rose up to sit round the house
Bidding farewell to heat caught in the walls
Rested their backs against red bricks, they did
All to swim in the radiating warmth
Papa is gone. Exit the solo. Enter the duet.
Togetherness unfolded to rise up and shine
Reversed was the insanity of myopia
Assented to by whisper of winds
and gaze of the laughing sun

Beckoning the duet to unsing
The songs he sang, shed tears
Of its Overloaded heart, kiss a carcass
Of such a tamed cobra
And mumble about thunder hidden in a storm
A flowery project projecting us to be poor
Now we all bark at a 'spirit'
Whose booming voice
Had flown up and down,
Shredding hearts of men,
Defeating lustful Desires
And silencing all mortals
In a grave, a frozen bunch of bones sleeps
On a razor blade of time,
With no whisky to clean his throat.
No perfume of power
Or chants about his glory befits him
A dry leaf is his name
Ready to be picked up by summer fires

Chikangaude

For Nancy Phiri

I
She sneaked into the compound
All smiles, dancing without a song
The nestlings called him 'Chikangaude,'
Mighty spider stirring dust from the depth
Of the paths: they ran, all of them, to her
Thudding of their bare feet, the rhythm
Of an African morning
Clapping of their hands, the sound
Of an African evening
The moment of joy to stressed faces
Clouds of dust filling the peaceful light
And, short nostrils blowing thick mucus
On the soil on which Chikangaude swings
The nestlings threw dirty coins-collected
From dry pockets of poor farmers-all to beg
The mighty spider to dance again; and
Dance she did.
The village shook to the wave
The torn minds start to mend
"Chikangaude, Chikangaude."

So they hailed her till the dawn of night
All nestlings refused to go home
Dances and more dances were their wish
And Chikangaude was their entertainer
Joy tickled their foggy faces
The blue sky sang in their horizon
God must live forever
He has brought Chikangaude to them
A saviour riding on wings of hope
A guest of all guests
'Mami Wota,'
A spirit of victory
A friend indeed
A timely thunder

II

At break of dawn
Chikangaude refuses to dance
Why, Chikangaude, why
It was only yesterday
Your drum-like voice
Travelled far and wide
Trees had swayed
And walls had fallen
Why must you freeze?
It was only yesterday
Your swinging body
Cat-walked into posh cars
Of our minds,
Pungent perfume of power
Chanted about your glory
You can't freeze now;
Greet us with a swollen face
Absorbing heat trapped in the walls
Of the bathroom
You can't greet us
With unkempt hair smiling, and
Droopy eyes dripping
Juices of anger

III

As wings
Of the morning flap away
Chikangaude opens her mouth:
'You were all happy
When my legs stretched higher and higher
And my hips swung like a spring
All those moments
No one gave me food to eat,
Water to drink and room to rest
In a tree, I slept
And when my limbs
Were broken, you all retired home
You left me, alone
Told you to sing about togetherness
But your lips hugged, alone sang I
Told you to dance the rain dance
Your legs glued, alone danced I
And no arm moved to a love dance
You come again today
And tell me, show us your dancing skills

How can we glorify the future
If all I say and do
You do not say and do?
Since you are alone at home
Bring your mother's new zitenje
All of you, one by one. Quickly.'

Soon after that;
And, in a chariot of dust
Chikangaude started to dance
Slowly, higher, slowly, higher
Until the clouds hid her forever

In pursuit of identity, integrity and patriotism

I

A monsoon is masturbating in the boudoir of the sky,
Soon sperms will scatter across to ease the long erection;
A reverse of burdens or a song of a long-awaited future.
Virgins will scramble for it to feed their 'tired' wombs
But whirlwinds and charcoal flames will soon dance on it;
Flash floods will upon them sing the end
Of a naturalized law rumbling like snoring of a pig
Partying on the back of unfettered freedom
Amid thunderclaps and flashes of light
Slithering in the forest of a very dark night.
Brother, I wouldn't think about writing you a letter
But with you, I can say what would be hidden to others
I know you wouldn't like to see danger dancing like minnows
Slouching in the under growths, but here it is and sleep I cannot.
The battle is won, and it is for this reason I must write this notelet
Be not blind. This is the truth.
You are alone bathing skeletons trapped in mud

Amid wagging of tongues of imps and swashbucklers
Who religiously, in the name of greed, milked you
Until in the middle of it when suddenly a red light
Smiled on your window. None is left except you.
You better bid beer bye so you don't see cogwheels
Instead of people that you speak to in a language
Of your choice. They are a by-product of bleeding hearts
And none of their hair is shaven for a purpose.
Dressed are their imbroglios and the field is a carpet
Of green grass. Beneath, their hearts are armed
But their faces suggest they love their rags.

II

All beautiful powerful trees face resistance
Yet have roots. In silence, shadows cover them,
And dew drops feed them.
Not all who bark are dogs.
Their calls are dents of black clouds
In the shadow of your name
You are the workshop that birthed them.
You can tow them or erect business centres, schools,
hospitals
Near them. Was on Mount Michesi last time to see

How well your bread was being buttered
Life was treating you well, and to prostitutes
Your short small snake softened. Adjust your life.

III
I sit at my veranda and stare at the sky
Before the gun starts to shoot the sperms
All ulcers of gluttony, of corruption
Of destitution howling dust and rocks, circumcise.
The down pour will blink and shy away
The earth's mouth will spit no laughter
Nor polish windscreens of whispers
In an oven of tears stirred in blood
This is home. Think twice, brother.
It's a blessing in disguise to be back in power.

The graveyard blinks in season

The face of the graveyard blinks
In season, blinks at scrawny babies
Strapped at the back of famished mothers
Baking in black sunlight.
A school of crows spread their wings
Into its mouth; their long shadows
Mouthing songs of victory,
Shoving their heads,
Craving for survival
Whose solutions lie in deaths
The face of the graveyard blinks,
Silently staring; its toothless mouth
Humming a fateful song
In defense of a virgin land
Replete with waves of dust
Whirling from caves of rust.
They are not at fault
Their sin is to be born here
And be prisoner not to see light
Always dozzing or grinning at their
Own tear-filled eyes, their giraffe-necks
Elongating to help them read
Names and count numbers
Of their enemies, too slow to see

What is amiss
They sculpt their eyebrows,
Twist their tongues for alms
Their faces drooping behind masks of gods,
Their front paws hidden in empty pockets,
Always staring
At passers-by's fat purses with gusto,
Saliva and sweat
Sinking down their white gowns

Disc of destiny

She walks into your life
Not as a star to shine
Alone in the sunlight
Nor fire fuelled by heat waves
To burn uncharted peace
But a disc of destiny
Detached from the sky
She walks in, soft-spoken,
Laughing at smelling streams
And hefty hills curved
In a valley of jealousy
She walks in, clothed in white
Ready to pump positive energy
Solid as a rock
Not a sheriff driven by greed,
An actor forced to perform
The roles of a wife
Stirred by theft
She walks in to plant
A ring on your finger
She's ready for you

To be truly yours forever
She's human just as you are
In an all-green tree,
Few yellow leaves brandish their teeth;
Lizards, tree snakes and bees
Shake hands in silence
And nobody talks about them
Because they are part of it
Just say 'My tree is beautiful.'
Looks like a fuzzy statement
To a puppy held by the scruff
Of its neck--
You obviously know
Certain things aren't right
But be still. That's for your eye
Just understand us--
Build a city in her heart
Make her always happy
And bring back beautiful babies
Food for thought for you
She walks in, and she's not afraid
Of insinuations and intimidations
And everything we speak about:
Those battles life offered you
Those wars you gallantly fought
Those worms that nibbled your

Late wives and children's
Flesh and finally their life
Those chunks of thorns
You harvested in humility
But unshakable as a statue
This girl, turning twenty
Tomorrow is really yours--
Away from us she looks
As Mganda dancers
Chant your names, roll in a circle,
Harness the beauty of love
Her beads glittering and beating
The curiosity of spectators
An evening light flashing
To persistent coughing of drums

Sleep child

The moon shines on our palms,
Lighting the placenta of sleeping memories,
Swishing of ill-thoughts
Chasing pitch darkness swelling
On the face of the parched earth
Small stones from the sky
Melt into drops of water on
Our Roofs to cool our burdensome hearts
Our bloody heels have knocked
Careless stones for ages
Shaking to the fright of
Changing seasons

The moon finally sets in the stomach
Of singing drums
In time for silence to return
Sleep child. Cry no more
Your mother will come
When the rooster 'cries' loud enough

Princess from the moon

Princess from the moon
You were born to glow
Glow on my face
The smell of chicken soup
Swings for every nose;
And only the fly runs fast
The beauty of a tall tree
Slaps every face;
And only the sawyer smiles first
The pimple hidden in a make-up
Itches; and only the owner knows
When to scratch it
Princess from the moon
You were born to fly
But it's not a must
That you fly everyday
Stay home, and be cool
Wash your 'dirty' hands
Look deeper beyond
The bleaking clouds
And soar slowly
Like a small chirping bird
And seal all holes
Smelling of cheap propaganda

And massage scars
Of worldly pleasures
You are not a love bank
In everlasting parties
Looking for strangers to hold you
You are not a lost bird perching
Everywhere, crying for easy ends
Forgetting the means
You were born to shine
The flesh of the apple
Is not as tasty as its face
The world is silently turning, turning
To sleep on the horns
Of a New order
And you not the queen of banks
Always touring long pockets of men
Spare a moment and listen to them, our elders
And you will not get a twinge
Dressed are flowers
Flowers are because of light
Nights are black
Black is because of soot
You will be soot dancing
In a dusty dream
In the shadow of your blindness

Springs of joy

When the vessel
Of love is filled
To the brim
My thoughts drown
In springs of joy
My joy leaps
In torrents of laughter
My laughter swims
In madness
When suddenly all efforts
Are lost to the wind

Love redefined

What is love
When the sweetness of a smile
Lasts only for a mile
When the beauty of lipstick
Is licked by a dose of lies
When beckoning of eyelids
Is bruised by morning blues
When the smell of roses
Is carried away by wind
When moulds grow on a health cake
And we choose to hide
When storms violently rage
And we do not kneel and pray
Love ought not be a thorn in the flesh

Postcard for Gumbi town

I would like to write a postcard for Gumbi town
Like a dustbin, the mouth
Of Gumbi town is no longer shut
Flies sing on its lips
Spiders build on the frames
Open day and night
Gumbi town swallows them
People: short and tall, smart and shabby
By bus, on foot: their cargo on their heads
Wrinkled faces, short slim hands, tall toes
As though limping from jaws of war

But when the door is wide open
Why not them into Gumbi town?
It is not full,
Seemingly, it will not be full
The M1 road that slices it
Thank God, it brings them while
Wasps dose at the entrance
Bees languidly buzz on its nose
And despairing peep at the passing commuters
Wave at them, at best, wishing them well
While teaching them new ways
Of committing crimes
And whispering crimes
That have never been committed

The weather has truly changed
Exposed are words of truth
Naked are our girls in market places
Telling it all that there is nothing to hide
Men do it on other men. Why
Not in Gumbi town

Clumpy creatures corrupting minds
Brain draining own folks
In the name of miracles and money
There is no grass in the river
All animals are feeding according
To their own zeal

The shepherd has fled
Telling it all that time is here
Brother must bake brother
Sister must swill sister
Nobodys must remain in their bodies
The world has truly changed

Driving own cars in Gumbi town
Must always carry cash for
Beggars that line the roads
Uniformed men, salaried men...
Gumbi town is a play
The cast has gone to sleep

Creaking hospital beds
Spitting frail patients
Pot-bellied men, fat-necked bourgeoisie
This is the land they built
Men of bright colours with a word
Everybody eye to the sky
Let us close our eyes to pray
That they may not be seen
In their birth suit

Jumping dams on dummy country roads
Like frogs
China cars squeal upon seeing another pothole
This is Gumbi town, why not
Half-baked pupils singing good-bye teacher
Innocently memorizing wrong formulae
For the one introducing them on the chalkboard
Either did not use them beyond what he tells
Or has other better pupils: sons of chiefs
Sons of politicians, daughters of the affluent
He must rush to attend to, why not

Preaching about change of mindset
Whose mindset? The mindset that old people
Are dambos that douse fire?
Or the mindset that poor people are tools?
Gumbi town is a play
The main character has forgotten his lines

Sitting at Changa CDSS with few resources
Spending sleepless nights visualizing a bright future
The university corridors are shut
The huge lock on it says 'money' you fool
Or return home and make babies
Gumbi University is not place for the pitiable

Afternoon is busy with mad crows
In bright fingernails and eyebrows
Black and white and black and red
Picking up rotten rats of Gumbi town
Crawling like creatures from long forgotten caves;
On the shops displaying their thighs
Waving at darkness, brandishing plump hips

Gumbi town is
Slowly packing, slowly rolling
Prematurely slipping from our hands
Water pipes weeping
Energy saver bulbs falling
Tipsy-turvy like overripe mangoes
Into merciless hands of dark nights

Going, everything is going
Their irritating skid marks shining
Black clouds blanketing the sky
Wind from southeast lazily trotting to the west
The morning light disappearing
Tears from the sky
Are snaking on the invisible cheeks of the atmosphere
Tall legs wetting the ground
In the west: dark with too much of it
In Gumbi town: light with scanty drops

Scruffy city children singing 'help boss, help boss'
Lifts my annoyance and takes me to Naperi Bridge
Mind lost, nose running like a broken pipe
I sit without any intention to lap
The cold water under it
Buzzing of motorcycles
And howling of trucks from Sanjika
Smother my frail ears and take me down town
Swimming in fine perfume, faces beaming with joy

No children songs would sing
Of refrigerators and cookers
I would open a bottle of coke
And drink half of it, and half of it throw away
I would take lunch box to school
And give to friends at a cost of a slap

Down the bridge, toads would scramble for food
I would throw a stone
They would swim away but
Suddenly return to it
I would laugh because I used to
Think they thought it was food
Young frogs dumped to fend for themselves

I returned to see children
Of somebody's children singing around Gumhi town
Their faces fluttered with innocence
Their hearts laden with the weight of hunger
Waving at motorcade meandering
In the city centre towards the airport
Take this postcard for my town
At a cost of no motivation at all, but shame

The dead end of a deadly dinosaur

I

Well, I remember you met
When things were falling apart
And the scars he left
Are still hidden in your heart
Him you cannot forget
On your wall he wrote
Chikutumbwe was here
On your thighs he tattooed
Chikutumbwe, Chikutumbwe
The inflicter of pain and sorrow
The sun scorching in ernest
The moon always following you home
The star hiding in clouds of dust
The worm swimming in heat
The duster erasing happiness
The broom fanning progress
I remember you defied all odds
Trotted away from the moonlight
To set open fires, the torch of an African night
For that's what you had to do
Before he broke blisters of your sleep
From snake and mosquito bites,
The song of African nights
He wagged his tail, and widened his mouth

To chase your hips.
You remembered there was a hyena
Blocking your paths not very long time before
Stealing all your new borns
Nibbling the very young shoots
Uprooting any of your strange thoughts
Your words, and your boldness
Empowered by free press
And dipping of fingers in an ink of wisdom
You chased him away
And all his eggs thrown
In a brick oven
Him, the dinosaur
Holding a flywhisk
Of liberty and freedom,
Uniting the broken hearts,
Mending soles of bleeding souls
Him, before he became deadly
Came but to salt your wounds,
Crack your frail bones
And sweep them into his huge belly
With four pails of milk
Why before the end of five years?
Weird songs wafting at break
Of dawn
Amid beating of drums;

Walking torches of grass
Lighting the estranged village
(In the wisdom of a rooster
Crying atop the tree)
You rang the bell:
'Wake up! Wake up! Wake up!
We said the hyena was bad
Oh, forgive us, Lord
This one is ten times bad
Wake up! wake up! wake up!
We said the hyena was bad
Oh, forgive us, Lord
This one is hundred
Times bad
Let's hunt him and
Remove his carnossial teeth!'

II

Tough-looking, giant and soft-spoken;
Chikutumbwe, the dinosaur
Readied himself to finish you
And saunter triumphantly to the next
Generation with just his own
Had a mouth, so wide
A tongue with tentacles like an octopus;
Whose cloud brought down a rain of saliva,
Whose gullet was cracked; but whistled

And, when he was swallowing his delicacy,
Blowing like that of a trumpet
Was heard from where he hid
Surrounded by Pulisi Chefu, the chief dog;
Amene Khomandu and Sajeni Fwipi,
The chief warthogs;
Khadata Kuala, the chief loyalist
And Jastasi Mwetu, the law keeper
Whose tongues were always out baying for blood;
Whose hands were busy scratching
Fat potbellies into which kachasu,
The bitter African drink sunk
Had a metal bowl; all dogs
Sneezed into it: his soup for the next day
Baby dogs were a dessert on his table,
That's why he kept female dogs
In the evening; remember
The Feast of Black Night

A bell was sounded
And Khadata Kuala and his loyalists assembled
To clap their paws, kowtow as he ate
And sing about his accomplishments in a parade:

Left, right!
Left, right!
Left, right!
No fear in that bush
No fear in that bush
We are
We are dinosaur's men
We are
We are dinosaur's men
We vow to bow
We vow to bow before him
No fear in that bush

About turn!
Right, left!
Right, left!
Right, left!

And soon after that,
Silence shook its waist
For him to inspect the parade
Basking in the glory of barefeet
As Pulisi Chefu wiped his mouth,
Amene Khumando bowed
And in a loud voice said:
'Long live Chikutumbwe!
No hand can touch your shoulder
Unless it is ready to die!'

The walls echoed, and
Chikutumbwe smiled
Towards midnight
Into his mouth, remember
That unfortunate piglet
And those pails of milk
And, nodding his head,
Chikutumbwe laughed and shouted:
'I hear they are coming
Let them come
Do not stop them
Their ominous hearts
Will betray them.'

III
I remember you stood
At ease an anthill
'We are being trapped
And soon we will be finished.
Wake up! wake up! wake up!
The hyena, two times bad
Chikutumbwe, hundred times badS
Wake up! wake up! wake up!

Chikutumbwe was too big
To catch the piglets
Who did the job for him?
Perhaps, Pulisi Chefu
But Pulisi Chefu

Could not say it was him
For he had never spoken
The truth. Ouch!
They gathered to mourn an empty coffin;
Just to sweep away
The misfortune
A game of tough minds
A job for big brains
A torch of truth
They gathered in one spirit
Mourning in the inconcreteness
Of their wisdom; their fingers tied
Together standing in a circle
Like an assembly of fragments
Brewing secrets of diving
Mastered by eagles

From a far catching fish
Drowned in a sea of joy
In the speed of pitch darkness
Only to be slapped by a sharp
Light coming from nowhere
They gathered, burying their shaved heads
Between their legs, the young and the old
Mourning an empty grave
Wasn't this madness while the real grave
Gaped at them? Ouch!
Brothers and sisters in pain
Swayed by whispers of terror
Moved by winds of slavery
Flattered by sadness of delight
Pulled by a rope of conscience
Stirred by a stick of a bitter root

At the summit of sleep
They were not asleep
At the summit of a festival
They were not blind
And they could freeze but
Could not be frozen
They were not dumb but

Could speak to one another
They woke up, in a single file
Arms at the back
Straight to the estranged village
Burying a banana tree
Wasn't this madness while
They knew their brother's body
Was crushed head to toe
And thrown into a pan by him?
Were they minions seductively
Looking at the moon's beauty
In the basin of water?

IV
If one of them betrayed a brother
Which they often thought
Who poisoned his heart to sell his own?
And if it was their Paramount Chief
Who would bell him?
In my Gumbi town, mortals
Lost in the music of their heart-beats;
Cheated by sweet songs of bad omen,
Slowed down by knocking of big blows
Greeted by scents of burning bush

Would around their homes
Erect fences of cactus shrubs,
Invite distillers of kachasu
And brewers of masese
Sacrifice a lamb under the big mpoza,
The tree of rain and water
In my Gumbi town, mortals
Stirred by groaning of blood,
Jostled by emptiness of joy,
Maddened by crying wombs
Slapped by fog of death cries
Weighed down by cowardice
Would on top of their roofs
Plant flags and talismans of the akafula
Calling for spirits of their ancestors
To take away Chikutumbwe, the monster
But these were piglets, their Paramount Chiefs
Love to be silenced with a cheap opium

V

Who said silence can impress?
Cats in my town sing miawo, miawo
Walking by the door of the kitchen
Watching the frying and souping
Of the slain big black cock
Which was waking them up
Early in the morning
Silence is night of the day

Could be hailed in the past
When all you said was heard
In a country without freedom of speech
Tied with strings of silence were lips
Bound in a sack of fresh sisal ropes;
Whipped, wounded and
Led into a pool of chitedze
On the head a cap of thorns
Nailed on the cross of darkness
Who said then silence can impress?
Silence wrapped in the twinkling of fear
Concocted by long thick chains of suffering
Driven by unnatural ways of handling peace
Isn't it a source of slavery and exploitation?
The piglets wouldn't be silent
The rest of their life
I remember once you had
A vigil. Hundred metres
Away from Pulisi Chefu's place
And you shouted:
'Stop killing us. Meet us if you are human.'

VI

Word was sent through fumes of sleep
Spinning in the beauty of dawn
Clothed in showers of dew
Like a young girl trotting away

From the watershed of love
Shuffling soles of tree tops
To reach the rifts of his sinews
The pigs are chanting
Spears, clubs and swords in hand
And stones and bags of sand
The writing on the wall is bold
And their tears wash their
Shadows gawking at singing trees
In silence, their forefathers spirits
Are limping
In their crutches, propping
Their trunks forward to meet him

VII

The big bell sounds in the arena
Shaking foundations of the ears of the world
Begging bolts and nuts to unscrew
And muscles of the earth to relax and contract
And all eyes to pivot or sing or
Shine like lights of the streets
Whose dust was washed away by whispers
And in your funeral cloth
Made of cotton of frustration
Cultivated in the dry season
Relevant for cultural songs and dance
Offering sacrifices by tattooing

Your bodies were in serious match
You were in serious match
Burning of wet wood full of smoke
Rising vertically and swinging in currents
Darkening the city
And blackening the black sky
The weak die
So many times
In their fear;
And though they walk
In the shadow of death
Empowered they are
All in black
Brandishing their biceps
Calling a spade a spade
Tell me, did you?

VIII

Questions failed the gums of the earth
And the mouth of its eyes
Did Chikutumbwe have ears to
Listen to the piglets' voice?
May be, the big task before him
Was too big to give up power
And announce peace back to the land
May be, the torture awaiting him
Was too massive to just say,
I have given up

May be, the fear in his mind
Was lack of peace wherever he wished to go
May be, the pride he nurtured
May be, the proof of his titles
May be, his cheeky wife;
May be, his bad reputation,
May be, the donations he stole,
And Pulisi Chefu
And Sajeni Fwipi
He was to leave behind
He tore off your petition
And waited for your next action

IX

You cried and cried and cried:
'Chikutumbwe must fall!
His wings must stop flying him beyond
Human thinking and imagination
His followers must see
What shaved a guineal fowl--
Master of Hope for the hopeless
No longer, he is. His power
Lies on the tongue like a flower
Sprouting on a candle flame
His energy is but lost to the wind
In the thick of arguments
His lawyers are a confused lot
Dunderheads, always jumping

Into flickering light
Buzzing bees justifying nothing
The root of his fall
Sweating faces, watery mouths
Unfolding nests of scorpions
Biting the game of fame
Blowing trumpets tearing his heart
Gradually remarking history scripts
And stirring hot pot of political porridge
Warming the umbilical cord of time;
The soul of freedom
Exploding cities of torn visions
Weaving poetry from weeping hills
Overlooking tall buildings away
From offices of snoring bosses.'

X

There is an ounce of reason
To the question
'Who eats the eaten?'
The piglets say they are being eaten
The Pulisi Chefu says it's not true;
The piglets to say such a thing are mad
Amene Khumando knows the truth;
And looks at Jastasi Mwetu
And silently watches the hullabaloo
Soberness thickening and tangling

Wounding and pounding;
Deleting and defeating
Grey chins overgrown
With ragwort and thistle
And wads of suscipicion
Stunned by excitement
And no wink of sleep
Amene Khumando knows it
And her feet hurting from high heels
On such a warm, still day
She smiles, the piglets
Are missing. Their mothers
Have to be compensated
By escorting all of them
To the Monsters house
Pleading for their safety
And beating Pulisi Chefu's boys
In song and dance:
Chikutumbwe must go!
Go! go! go!
Chikutumbwe must go!
Go! go! go!
Chikutumbwe must go!
For peace to reign
XI
Aaaaaah! Asah!
Pandemonium at the Monsters house
And Amene Khumando watches!

The truth unheard of
Nipping out of bed
Of grass on a windswept hungry
Hill guarded by flags of banana
Leaves keeping the sun from
Fading the bright colours
Of his glory, Chikutumbwe
Stands three metres high; and
Sounds the bell himself:
'Asaah!
Amene Khumando!
Amene Khumando!
Why do you escape from my palms
And choose to become a traitor!
Sajeni Fwipi rise!
Sajeni Fwipi rise!
Pulisi Chefu!
All dogs to the streets!
Amene Khumando down!

XII

Loud songs on the streets;
'Amene Khumando must fall!
The traitor must go!
Amene Khumando must fall!
The traitor must go!'
Jogging the zestful dogs
Led by Pulisi Chefu

And on the Feast of Black Night
Amene Khumando's life was taken
Who, everybody wonders,
Was Amene Khumando to betray him
And say Chikutumbwe must go
He who doesn't have a country to run?
By feeding on the majority;
Disallowing them a peaceful sleep of death,
Sending the minority on forced leave
Hang his peace, doesn't he?

XIII
My friend, Jastasi Mwetu!
My friend, Jastasi Mwetu!
Innocent blood bark in bare hills
The laws of the land
Are the synovial fluid
In the caves of your bones
And though you eat on his table
The scroll of justice
Is clear on infringements of rights
Not on the cover and the blurb
But in the language--
The scroll is in the language
Of the pigs--a thing Chikutumbwe hates
If you cannot, the pigs are nothing
Jastasi Mwetu! Jastasi Mwetu!
Save the pigs, Jastasi Mwetu!

XIV

A baffling noise under his skin
Reminiscent of a plane take-off
And canals of sweat
Splashing blood of death
Jastasi Mwetu drums justice
He must save the pigs
Or die soothing his conscience
The pigs have but a strong case
Jastasi Mwetu knows the truth
And must save the pigs
Chikutumbwe has a kraal
In the sanctuary of the pigs
He must go to prison for his sins
Yet Chikutumbwe has power
To have the law twisted
And have all pigs silenced
In prison of a belly
Jastasi Mwetu drums justice
Pools and pools of sweat
The strings of justice
Speaking to his nerves
Khadata Kuala and his loyalists
Inserting pins inside his eye
To make a metal ball
Out of clay
Or steal a corn

While the farmer is watching
Jastasi Mwetu drums justice

XV
My friend, Khadata!
My friend, Khadata!
Why do you say
Mwetu's justice is no justice?
Why do you throw tantrums?
The walls of the house
Drips blood
The laws of the land
Are the backbone of power
You forced me to study and study
Open pages and pages
Spend nights and nights
Was it to remove the whiskers
Of philosophical part of the law
And disappoint the best poetry of it?
Law is law
How can you fight against it?
Chikutumbwe has power
But he is not above the law
Stand by my side
The piglets must be in peace

XVI

My friend, Sajeni Fwipi!
My friend, Khadata Kuala!
Echoes whispers of blood-shed
Stand by my side
These piglets are not at fault
Why should they be killed?
You are the only ones
Who understand the law
Tell Chikutumbwe
To repent his sins
And go to prison
Life will be better there
Than kill and kill and kill
And shed more blood
His days are numbered

XVII

And you saw it;
The gasping
The dizzy
The unseen pain
The sins committed
The blaze in the eye
The fire in the mouth
The blinking of the eyelids
The wave of scorn
The stolen warmth
And no more
Feasts of Black Night